My First Bible Verses

Finger Plays for God's Word

Christine Suguitan

Illustrated by Nancy Munger

CPH
SAINT LOUIS

Genesis 28:15

I

(*Point to yourself.*)

am with you

(*Touch your palms to your shoulders.*)

3

and will watch over you

(*Shield your eyes with a hand; look left and right.*)

wherever you go.

(*Walk your fingers in a wide circle.*)

Psalm 9:2

I
(*Point to yourself.*)

will be glad
(*Grin.*)

and rejoice
(*Raise your arms and happily jump up.*)

in You.
(*Point up.*)

Lord, You

(*Point up.*)

will keep us safe

(*Hug yourself.*)

and protect us.

(*Shelter your head with your arms.*)

The Lord

(*Point up.*)

is my

(*Point to yourself.*)

strength.

(*Flex your arm muscles.*)

You

(*Point up.*)

are my

(*Point to yourself.*)

King

(*Trace a crown on top of your head.*)

and my God.

(*Place a hand over your heart.*)

My mouth

(*Point to your mouth.*)

is filled

(*Raise your arms overhead.*)

with Your praise.

(*Lift one hand in praise; place the other hand over your heart.*)

Worship the Lord

(*Look up as you fold your hands.*)

with gladness;

(*Clap your hands.*)

come before Him

(*Move your arms toward yourself in a "come here" gesture.*)

with joyful

(*Clap your hands.*)

songs.

(*Move your arms as if to conduct singers.*)

Trust

(*Thump your chest gently with a fist.*)

in the Lord

(*Point up.*)

with all

(*Stretch your arms out wide.*)

your heart

(*Place a hand over your heart.*)

and lean not

(*Lean to one side.*)

on your own understanding.

(*Tap your forehead.*)

Here am I.

(*Point to yourself.*)

Send me!

(*Point forward.*)

Do not

(*Shake a finger back and forth.*)

fear;

(*Clutch your shoulders and tremble.*)

I

(*Point to yourself.*)

will help you.

(*Stretch out your hands as if to offer help.*)

Isaiah 64:8

We

(*Point to yourself and others.*)

are the clay,

(*Wrap your arms around yourself and huddle like a ball of clay.*)

You

(*Point up.*)

are the potter.

(*Mold one fist in your other hand.*)

Jeremiah 33:3

Call to Me

(*Cup your hands around your mouth.*)

and I will

(*Place a hand on your chest.*)

answer you.

(*Pretend to hold a phone to your ear.*)

Love

(*Hug yourself.*)

the Lord

(*Point up.*)

your God

(*Point to others.*)

with all

(*Stretch your arms out wide.*)

your

(*Point to others.*)

heart.

(*Clasp your hands over your heart.*)

Mark 1:17

Come,

(*Stretch your arms forward in an inviting motion.*)

follow Me

(*Cup a hand and motion for someone to follow.*)

and I

(*Point to yourself.*)

will make you

(*Point to others.*)

fishers

(*Pretend to cast a fishing line.*)

of men.

(*Sweep your arm as if indicating many people.*)

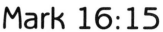

Go

(*Point forward.*)

into all

(*Stretch your arms out wide.*)

the world

(*Form a circle with your arms overhead.*)

Mark 16:15

and preach

(*Point up and look out at an imaginary crowd.*)

the good news

(*Look happily at your hands cupped to form a "Bible."*)

to all creation.

(*Sweep your arms in a circle.*)

Luke 11:1

Lord,

(*Point up.*)

teach us

(*Point an index finger as if making a point.*)

to pray.

(*Bow your head, close your eyes, fold your hands.*)

For God

(*Point up.*)

so-o-o

(*Stretch your arms out wide.*)

loved

(*Clasp your hands over your heart.*)

the world

(*Form a circle with your arms overhead.*)

that He gave

(*Stretch your arms forward.*)

His one

(*Hold up one finger.*)

and only

(*Hug yourself tightly.*)

Son.

(*Point up.*)

John 14:6

I am

(*Point to yourself.*)

the way

(*With palms together and thumbs up, "drive" your hands down a winding path.*)

and the truth

(*Stand at attention with a hand over your heart.*)

and the life.

(*Spring up, happily throwing your arms in the air.*)

I

(*Point to yourself.*)

chose you …

(*Point to another person.*)

to go

(*Point forward.*)

and bear fruit.

(*Stretch your arms like branches; cup your hands for "fruit."*)

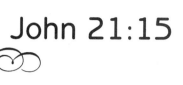

Jesus said …

(*Point up.*)

"Feed

(*Pretend to hand out food.*)

My

(*Point to yourself.*)

la-a-ambs."

(*Hold your hands at the sides of your head for ears. Bleat while saying "lambs."*)

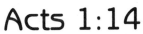

They all

(*Stretch your arms out wide.*)

joined together

(*Clasp your hands together.*)

constantly

(*Roll your arms.*)

in prayer.

(*Hold your palms together as if praying.*)

We

(*Point to yourself, then others.*)

cannot help

(*Shrug with your palms up.*)

speaking

(*Move the fingers and thumb of one hand together and apart.*)

about what we have seen

(*Point to an eye.*)

and heard.

(*Point to an ear.*)

1 Corinthians 15:3–4

Christ died for our sins …

(*Stretch out your arms as if on a cross.*)

He was buried …

(*Lay your arms together to one side.*)

He was raised

(*Raise up your arms from the buried position. Smile.*)

on the third day.

(*Hold up three fingers.*)

1 Corinthians 16:13

Be on your guard;

(*Stand at attention and salute.*)

stand firm

(*Stand with your legs apart, arms crossed firmly over your chest.*)

in the faith.

(*Clasp your hands over your heart.*)

2 Corinthians 9:7

God

(*Point up.*)

loves

(*Hug yourself.*)

a cheerful

(*Point to your smile.*)

giver.

(*Stretch your open hands in front of you.*)

Galatians 5:13

Serve

(*Stretch your arms forward.*)

one another

(*Point to one another.*)

in love.

(*Hug yourself.*)

Ephesians 4:32

Be kind …

(*Clasp your hands over your heart.*)

to one

(*Point to yourself.*)

another.

(*Point to others.*)

1 Peter 5:7

He

(*Point up.*)

cares

(*Rock your arms.*)

for you.

(*Point to others.*)

Revelation 7:17

God will

(*Point up.*)

wipe away

(*Move your arm in a sweeping motion.*)

every

(*Point at spots in front of you.*)

tear from their eyes.

(*Pretend to wipe tears from your eyes.*)

Hints for Teachers and Parents

In His Word, God reveals His plan for our salvation through the death and resurrection of His Son. Finger plays are a powerful tool for implanting Scripture in young minds. They supply the repetition and fun young children love.

Show your love for God and His Word as you speak the verses. Speak slowly, timing the motions with the words. Make your movements expansive and simple. Simplify the motions and verses for very small children or children with a disability.

Take a moment to talk with the children about the meaning of the verses. You will be following Jesus' command to feed His lambs!

Here are a few ideas for using the verses in school or at home.

❋ *Devotions.* Act out and discuss one or two finger plays as part of your family devotions or as a lesson supplement with toddlers.

❋ *Story time.* Read through and act out a number of finger plays for a bedtime or read-along story.

❋ *Verse of the week.* Choose one verse to learn and review all week. Say and act out the verse at school during prayer time and at home when saying grace.

❋ *Break time.* Use a finger play at school (or home) when children need a refreshing break, or when you want to fill an extra minute with a meaningful activity.

❋ *Games.* Let older children see how quickly they can remember and act out a verse. Act out a verse silently and see if your child can guess the words.

❋ *Music.* Play rhythm instruments or clap while saying

the words. Make up simple melodies for the words.

✳ *Recording.* Make an audio or video recording of the children acting out the verses. Let them hear and/or see themselves in action.